The Beauty of Lost Places

Cornelia Kaufmann

The Beauty of Lost Places

Presentation by *BookLeaf Publishing*

Web: www.bookleafpub.com

E-mail: info@bookleafpub.com

ISBN: 9789358313215

First edition 2024

To everyone actively helping and protecting Mother Earth.

Autumn Leaves

In the hush of autumn's whispered sigh,
leaves cascade, a tapestry from the sky.
A palette of gold, crimson, and rust,
nature's masterpiece, shimmering in the dusk.

Crisp whispers echo in the woodland glades,
as leaves descend in the arboreal parades.
Dancing with the wind in a farewell waltz,
nature's tapestry unravels, the season exalts.

Amber-gilded whispers, a forest's serenade,
as leaves embark on a journey, a symphony played.
Rustling secrets in the cool, crisp air,
autumn leaves descend, watched by a hare.

Each leaf, a storyteller of summer's embrace,
now flutters down with delicate grace.
Carried by the breeze, a gentle ballet,
autumn leaves pirouette, then gently lay.

The trees stand bare, their branches exposed,
yet beauty lingers, in the leaves composed.
A mosaic on the earth, a mosaic on the breeze,
autumn's surrender, a chorus among the trees.

Underneath the canopy, a rustling carpet lies,
whispers of a season bidding goodbyes.
Nature's confetti, a celebration untold,

in the tapestry of autumn, stories unfold.

Leaves, once emerald, now ablaze in descent,
a symphony of colours, a vivid lament.
Yet in their fall, a promise to renew,
in the cycle of seasons, life continues.

So let the autumn leaves weave their tale,
of transformation, resilience, and trails.
In their descent, a lesson to glean,
nature's poem, etched in foliage no longer green.

Muddy Feet

Beneath the canopy of ancient trees,
muddy trails wind through the mysteries.
Earth's embrace, a squelchy ballet,
in the heart of the wild, where wanderers stray.

Mud-laden footprints, a story they tell,
of journeys taken, where the wild spirits dwell.
Each squish and slurp, a rhythmic song,
on the muddy trails where we all belong.

The trail unfolds, a canvas of brown,
speckled with memories, up and down.
Raindrop percussion, a woodland symphony,
muddy trails echo with nature's harmony.

In the mud, secrets of the forest are kept,
a trodden path where creatures crept.
Squelching steps, a dance with the earth,
on muddy trails, where all find their worth.

Boots adorned with tales of the trail,
muddy imprints, a memoir unveiled.
A testament to resilience and wanderlust,
on the muddy trails, where dreams combust.

Through puddles and rivulets, the path meanders,
a testament to life's intricate candour.
Muddy trails, a metaphor for the soul,
navigating challenges to reach the goal.

So embrace the mud, its primal appeal,
on the muddy trails, where realities kneel.
For in each squelch and every stride,
lies the essence of life's muddy ride.

Gold on Sapphire

Upon the canvas of the horizon wide,
where the sky and sea in tender hues confide,
The ocean spreads its endless, liquid grace,
a symphony of azure, a boundless embrace.

Beneath the canvas of the celestial dome,
the sun, a golden sovereign, finds its home.
Its warm fingers reach, a touch so kind,
igniting sapphire waves, a shimmering bind.

The ocean whispers in a language unknown,
tales of seafarers and of adventures they own.
Each wave, a story in the grand expanse,
a dance of tides in an eternal trance.

Golden sunbeams kiss the cresting waves,
a radiant glow on the watery graves.
Sapphire hues, a reflection of the sky,
in this liquid realm, where dreams amplify.

Salty zephyrs carry the sun's soft hymn,
as gulls traverse the horizon's rim.
Seascapes painted in the palette of the day,
golden sun on sapphire waves at play.

Beneath the surface, a world unseen,
where coral gardens in splendour convene.
The sun's golden touch penetrates the blue,
illuminating secrets in the ocean's view.

As daylight wanes, and the sun descends,
a kaleidoscope of colours, a beauty transcends.
On the horizon's edge, where day meets night,
the ocean glows with a soft, golden light.

In this maritime ballet, where time behaves,
the sun sets golden on sapphire waves.
A celestial dance, a moment to savour,
by the ever-changing, eternal sea's behaviour.

The View From Grandma's House

There used to be a field at the bottom of the lane,
you could see it from every floor at grandma's house.
Houses, hedges, and wide open meadows, with nothing in your way,
across hills and valleys and forests until you saw the church steeple of the next town.

We sat by the window often,
making out landmarks in the distance.
Admiring the unobstructed view, no light pollution over cattle paddocks.
Just fields and forests and no trace of human life.

There was a secret shortcut that every kid knew,
across the top of the field.
Walking home from school I'd leave the road and continue on the footpath,
past the hedge at the bottom of the lane and around the corner
to rejoin civilisation a few doors down from grandma's house.

I used to sit on the fence and daydream in the sun,
wondering what animals I would encounter that day.
Sometimes I'd feed the sheep,
sometimes I'd get chased by cows.

There was a hidden gate, in the hedge.
It had been there since my grandma was a child.
If you knew where it was, you could be at the field within a minute
if you walked to the bottom of the lane and carried on straight to the little gap in the hedge.

Across from grandma's house was an orchard;
backing onto old, big gardens,
greenery as far as you could see
until your gaze hit the city centre high-rises.

We'd sneak into the orchard sometimes to steal apples
the old lady who owned it always grumpy, chasing us with a broom
but offering up fallen fruits for the entire neighbourhood to take
grandma's pies never tasted better.

Humans encroached on the empty field and the orchard.
One summer there was a meadow, and by autumn there was a house.
Gone is the hedge and the footpath at the bottom of the lane,
gone is the view across valleys and forests.

The orchard is long gone too, in its place new buildings and family homes

and I never noticed how narrow the street was that
grandma lived on,
until the fruit trees were replaced by concrete walls.
The city came closer until you could just make out
the church from the top floor window.

Grandma's house is gone, torn down to make space
for apartment blocks that don't belong.
The irony is that even that new penthouse suite now
in its place
will never have such a marvellous view
of the open field, valleys, forests, and orchard, that I
used to have from grandma's house.

In memory of Landhausstrasse 1, where I grew up.

Guardian Of The Heather

In the heart of the Scottish Highlands, where the heather blooms,
a stag, regal and wild, moves through the ancient gloom.
Majestic antlers, a crown of nature's design,
in the tapestry of hills, where the earth and sky entwine.

Amidst the rolling hills, a dance of purple and green,
he strides with grace, a creature seldom seen.
His hooves touch the earth, in rhythm with the breeze,
in the symphony of nature, he finds he’s at ease.

Heather waves in reverence, a carpet beneath his feet,
a sanctuary where silence and wilderness meet.
Eyes watchful, deep pools reflecting the moorland's lore,
in the solitude of the highlands, amongst legends of yore.

A whisper in the wind, tales of ancient clans,
of warriors and poets, in the stag's noble stance.
Through mist-kissed valleys and craggy peaks,
the stag roams free, cloaked in an air of mystique.

Amidst the rugged beauty, a harmony unfolds,
nature's secrets in the heather, a story untold.

Seasons change, a cycle that eternally weaves,
in the heart of the highlands, a stag among evergreen leaves.

Through warm amber sunlight and the silver moon's embrace,
the stag roams on, a symbol of untamed grace.
Guardian of the heather, keeper of the land,
in the Scottish Highlands, where wild dreams stand.

As twilight paints the sky in hues of purple and gold,
the stag lingers on, his silhouette brave and bold.
He carries the spirit of the moorland, untethered,
in the heathered hills, where nature and magic are gathered.

Free Spirit

Sun is glowing golden on the wheat
as riders on their horses take their seat.
The morning air in a cool, fresh breeze,
as strong hooves make their way with ease.

Along the fields and forest paths
from shadow into sunshine, away from the noisy
bypass.
Rider and horse become one
as they gallop into the rising sun.

Where to walk, trot, canter is known by heart
by both horse and rider, who together start.
Round the corner and muscular legs spring into
action
both knowing what to do through silent conversation.

In fields of gold, beneath the sun's bright shield,
the wind's embrace, a dance on hooves revealed.
With every stride, a rhythm wild and free,
galloping souls, in nature's symphony.

The earth beneath, a canvas vast and green,
where dreams take flight, and stories yet unseen.
The rush of air, a whisper through the grass,
as hoofbeats mark the time, the moments pass.

Each leap, each bound, a testament of grace,
a timeless chase in this enchanted space.
for in this field, where hearts and dreams roam,
horse and rider's spirits and freedom are at home.

Nani Pua

In the garden of Aloha, where trade winds gently sway,
Hawaiian flowers bloom in a vibrant display.
Each petal whispers tales of the tropical breeze,
a symphony of colours beneath the island trees.

🌺 Hibiscus, regal in hues so bright,
Crimson, coral, and sunshine ignite.
The state's floral crown, in gardens they sing,
in the heart of Hawai'i, eternal spring.

🌸 Plumeria, fragrant with a sweet perfume,
leis of white petals, a tropical bloom.
Underneath the moonlight, by the ocean's embrace,
in fragrant whispers, they dance with grace.

🌼 Yellow hibiscus, a golden sunbeam,
reflecting the warmth of a tropical dream.
In the garden's embrace, where stories are sown,
a blossom of joy, in shades of their own.

🌺 Bird of Paradise, a regal dancer's pose,
orange and blue, where the aloha spirit flows.
In the lush valleys and by the volcanic shore,
they beckon with grace, forevermore.

🌸 Orchids, delicate and drenched in hues,
in hidden valleys, covered the morning dew.

Aloft in the rainforest, where magic resides,
in the tapestry of flora, where beauty abides.

Tiare, the scent of Polynesian nights,
in moonlit gardens, where dreams take flights.
Petals pure, like the island's heart,
in the fragrant mosaic, Hawai'i's flower art.

Ginger blossoms, torches in the mist,
red and pink, where the trade winds assist.
In the tropical air, their secrets unfold,
in the embrace of Hawai'i, a paradise untold.

Beneath the Hawaiian sun, where the flowers bloom,
a kaleidoscope of colours, an island's perfume.
In each petal, a story of love to share,
Hawaiian flowers, a lei of aloha to wear.

Lava Flow

In the heart of the Earth's bold embrace,
lava pulses, a liquid fire's race.
A molten dance, an ancient trance,
in the belly of creation, where elements enhance.

Viscous rivers beneath the crust,
lava's journey, an unbridled thrust.
Crimson veins through obsidian dreams,
in the volcanic forge, where chaos teems.

An experimental ballet, a fiery art,
lava's movements, a choreography apart.
The dance of atoms, the ballet of heat,
in the liquid embrace, where energies meet.

Silken whispers of the cooling flow,
lava's tale, in the afterglow.
Upon solid ground, the story's etched,
a chronicle of heat, where the Earth's heart's fetched.

From the belly of mountains, a fiery birth,
lava spills, an elemental mirth.
A canvas of magma, a painter's delight,
in the subterranean gallery, where shadows alight.

Cracks and crevices, where lava creeps,
in the restless Earth, where passion seeps.
An experimental poem, in volcanic ink,
a testament to forces, where the restless think.

In the quiet aftermath, cooled and still,
lava's memory, etched on the hills.
A geological sonnet, a verse in stone,
in the silent echoes, where the fiery poem is known.

The Last Of His Kind

In memory of Solitario Jorge, better known as Lonesome George, the last Pinta Island Tortoise, who died in 2012 over 100 years old at the Charles Darwin Research Centre in Puerto Ayora, Isla Santa Cruz, Ecuador. I had the privilege of briefly working with him in 2007 as I was interning with the Parque Nacional Galápagos.

In the Galápagos, where ocean breezes sigh,
Lonesome George, under the equatorial sky.
A guardian of time on Pinta's shore,
shell of history, a relic to adore.

Solitude his companion on the golden sand,
last of his kind, in a dwindling band.
A traveller through epochs, ancient and grand,
in the whispers of waves, on the lonely strand.

A reptilian ambassador, a living sage,
on the isle of Pinta, in an endless cage.
Carapace worn like a weathered tome,
in the currents of time, where memories roam.

A tale told in the contours of his shell,
centuries of stories, the ocean could tell.
On the shores of extinction, he stood alone,
Lonesome George, a kingdom overthrown.

Eyes like constellations, reflecting the past,
echoes of companionship, too fleeting to last.

The echo of Darwin’s footfalls, now just a trace,
Lonesome George, the last of his race.

In the Galápagos, where time stood still,
a testament to nature's unyielding will.
A sombre ballad, a mournful dirge,
for Lonesome George, the last Pinta surge.

Yet, in his solitude, a legacy thrives,
a call to preserve, so life survives.
A century old, Pinta on his mind,
Lonesome George, the last of his kind.

Climate Change

In the book of the seasons, where tales unfold,
a chapter stained, by a story yet untold.
Upon the canvas of Earth, a subtle dance,
a pas de deux with fate, a climatic trance.

Spring, once adorned in hues of vibrant green,
now dons a coat, where warmth and chill convene.
Blossoms hesitant, as if in whispered fear,
for climate change, a subtle, looming tear.

Summer's embrace, once fiery and bold,
now bears the weight of stories yet untold.
Sunsets aflame, yet a hint of distress,
as Earth whispers secrets, a plea to confess.

Autumn leaves, in their dance to the ground,
speak of shifting winds, a subtle sound.
Harmony disrupted, a discordant refrain,
as climate change conducts a symphony of pain.

Winter's frost, a fragile, transient sheen,
yet beneath the ice, a world unseen.
Polar echoes of a warming tale,
as glaciers weep, their ancient story frail.

The seasons, once a predictable rhyme,
now dance to the beat of a changing clime.
Spring's arrival, delayed or hastened by degrees,
as climate whispers secrets to the budding trees.

Summer’s fervour, a touch too intense,
as heatwaves dance, in nature's defence.
The sun, a furnace in the endless sky,
yet beneath its rays, the ecosystems sigh.

Autumn's tapestry, once painted with ease,
now tangled threads, caught in a fickle breeze.
The colours blur, a canvas in disarray,
as climate change dictates a different display.

Winter's chill, a hesitant refrain,
as snowflakes ponder, to fall or wane.
The cold, a shiver in the changing air,
as climate murmurs, a warning, a dare.

In this intricate waltz of Earth and sky,
climate change whispers, a silent, subtle cry.
A dance disrupted, a rhythm distressed,
in the arms of seasons, the planet is caressed.

Yet hope lingers in the lingering mist,
a chance for change, a climate to resist.
For in the ballet of seasons, a tale untold,
the power to rewrite, in our hands, we hold.

The Legend Of The Gille Dubh

In the Highland shadows where legends tread,
dwells the Gille Dubh, a creature seldom said.
A guardian of the glens, a phantom in the night,
cloaked in mystery, veiled in twilight.

Black as the night, with eyes aglow,
in the moonlit moors, he treads soft and slow.
Silent whispers weave tales untold,
of the Gille Dubh, in the Highlands‘ fold.

A sprite of darkness, with mischief in his eye,
he weaves through heather 'neath the midnight sky.
Cunning and sly, in the forest he'll hide,
a creature of secrets, in the shadows bide.

He guards the ancient woods, where spirits roam,
a spectral warden, a guardian of home.
With mossy hair and a cloak of green,
in the heart of nature, but never seen.

Yet, fear not the Gille Dubh's enigmatic gaze,
for in Highland folklore, he dances in the maze.
A sprite of balance, of mischief and care,
in the sacred silence, he's always there.

In the rustling leaves and the babbling brook,
hear the tales of the Gille Dubh, in every nook.
A creature of twilight, a keeper of lore,
in the Highland shadows, forevermore.

Garden Haikus

Sage in wisdom's scent,
rosemary weaves thyme's embrace,
herb trio's dance.

Herbs on silent breeze,
aromatic dance unfolds,
nature's spice whispers.

Wildflowers in bloom,
nature's paintbrush, colours swoon,
wind whispers their tale.

Earth's cradle awaits,
potting soil in hands' embrace,
seeds dream of green fate.

Verdant carpet rolls,
sunlight kisses blades of green,
lawn's soft embrace calls.

Blossoms nod in breeze,
earth's canvas blooms with life,
garden whispers peace.

Buzz of wings, soft hums,
critters play in leafy realms,
nature's dance unfolds.

Purple whispers sway,
lavender breathes in the breeze,
aromatic grace.

Busy bees hum near,
flowers offer sweet nectar,
honey their reward.

Smoke Signals

Beneath the sable shroud of urban sprawl,
where progress hums, and factories bawl,
A tale unfolds of nature's silent plea,
in the shadow of progress, a symphony.

Rivers, once pure, now bear a heavy toll,
as pollutants drift, an insidious scroll.
A lament sung by the whispering reeds,
in the water's lament, a tragedy proceeds.

Smokestacks pierce the cerulean sky,
exhaling toxins, where the swallows fly.
A cacophony of industry, a discordant tune,
as the Earth sighs beneath the growing dune.

Plastic seas, where waves should kiss the shore,
polymer tides, an unwanted encore.
Nature's canvas marred by human hands,
in the plastic tide, pollution stands.

In the concrete jungle, where progress prevails,
the air holds particles, as silent gales.
A canopy of smog, a toxic haze,
as the earth's lungs struggle in a desperate daze.

Yet, amidst the gloom, a rallying cry,
a call to action beneath the tainted sky.
For in every polluted drop and every tainted breath,
there lies the power to stave off nature's death.

Let us weave a tapestry of change,
in the face of pollution, let hope arrange.
For every conscious choice, a seed to sow,
in the symphony of Earth, let harmony grow.

So, hear the plea in the rustling leaves,
feel the pulse in the ocean heaves.
In our hands, the power to restore,
a balance in nature, forevermore.

Woodpecker's Elegy

Dedicated to the ivory-billed woodpecker, a critically endangered species, last sighted in 1987 and listed as "definitely or probably extinct" since 2021.

In the annals of time, where shadows roam,
a creature once danced, now lost in the gloam.
Whispers of its presence, echoes in the air,
a lament for the one no longer there.

In a distant age, where the wilderness thrived,
a majestic creature, its essence derived.
A symphony of life in a vibrant refrain,
now silenced, gone, no longer to reign.

Amidst emerald forests and rivers that wend,
the Ivory-Billed Woodpecker, a legend to mend.
Wings adorned with ebony and a crimson crest,
in the realm of shadows, it found its nest.

A master of flight, through the timber it soared,
a guardian of secrets, ancient and stored.
In the heart of the swamp, where mosses entwine,
the woodpecker thrived, in a world so divine.

Yet, the winds of change, relentless and cold,
swept through the woodland, a story untold.
Habitats dwindled, echoes of chainsaw's wail,
the woodpecker's dance, replaced by a silent trail.

In the stillness of the forest, a void remains,
a whisper of wings, a chorus of refrains.
Silent beaks and a vacant gaze,
the Ivory-Billed Woodpecker, lost in the maze.

But let not the silence muffle its song,
in our hearts, the memory strong.
For in this elegy, a vow to defend,
the treasures of nature, on which life depends.

In the echoes of extinction, a plea resounds,
a call to stewardship, on fertile grounds.
For every creature gone, a part of us too,
in the tapestry of life, may compassion renew.

The Flood

For centuries the river valleys were alive with
industry.
Heavy grindstones turning with the river's might
man mastering nature.
Mills, workshops, polishers
all found along the shore,
one next to the other, door to door.
Canals hewn to divert the river's course
turning waterwheels to grind blades
like our great-grandfathers did.
But water is patient, and the river does not forget
and reclaims its course
over and over again.
Restaurants were workshops once stood,
sandbags in the door
wet feet, wet flooded basements.
The river, normally a pleasant brook
turns into whitewater after the slightest bit of rain
bursting its banks as it has always done.
But man does not learn
that the water always wins.
Stubbornly holding onto land won from the river
centuries ago.
Flood of the century they called it
the river swelling, dams overflowing
and man in the middle, surprised to drown.
Weirs now dry, canals no longer in use
the river reclaimed its course

always taking a bit of shoreline with it.

But man won't learn.

In memory of the devastating floods in Germany on 14th July 2021, including the river Wupper bursting its banks in Solingen.

Ancient Guidance

Beneath the canopy of ancient dreams,
where echoes of the past weave timeless streams,
Indigenous hearts beat in rhythm with the land,
a resilient pulse, steadfast, hand in hand.

In sacred groves where whispers linger,
wisdom passed down, fingers trace the singer.
Cultures rooted, intertwined with soil,
in every sacred step, a resilient coil.

Through the drumbeat of a thousand years,
resounds the resilience that conquers fears.
Modern winds may blow, a relentless tide,
yet indigenous spirits, forever abide.

In dances painted with ochre and grace,
they tread the Earth, leaving no hasty trace.
Harmony woven in every sacred song,
a testament to where they belong.

Oh, custodians of the ancient lore,
guardians of wisdom from days of yore,
Against the tide of progress and might,
Indigenous souls stand firm, shining bright.

Their languages, a symphony of the past,
resilient echoes that forever last.
Against the currents of change, they stand,
defenders of Earth, the native band.

Through struggles fierce, and battles won,
they dance with the moon, salute the sun.
Ceremonies woven in threads of time,
their resilience, a melody, a sublime chime.

Adorned in stories etched in the soil,
Indigenous roots burrow, coil by coil.
In every seed they sow, a promise sown,
a harmonious connection, deeply known.

Though skyscrapers rise and engines hum,
Indigenous spirits reverberate like a drum.
For in the heart of each sacred birth,
resilience thrives, a dance with Earth.

So let the winds of change attempt to blow,
through ancient groves where the spirits grow.
Indigenous souls, a beacon in the night,
guiding us back to a harmonious light.

Magic Fire In The Sky

In the heart of the Arctic, where silence lies deep,
there's a dance of colours, secrets it keeps.
From emerald greens to a shimmering blue,
the heavens ignite, painting stories anew.

Magic fire in the sky, dancing high and wide,
whispers of the ancients, where dreams coincide.
Oh, magic fire in the night, painting tales so bright,
in the dance of the northern lights, everything feels
right.

Legends speak of spirits, of warriors bold,
of tales untold, from the days of old.
Celestial ribbons, in a cosmic ballet,
moving, swirling, in the night's grand display.

Hear the whispers of the elders, in the cold wind's
sigh,
guiding souls, watching over, as the lights fly by.
To the rhythm of the tundra, where the reindeer roam,
the magic fire calls, drawing hearts back home.

To gaze upon this wonder, is to touch the divine,
a celestial spectacle, in a frozen shrine.
For in this fleeting moment, time seems to stand still,
captured by the beauty, an eternal thrill.

Ancient songs, sung by the stars, echo through the
night,
telling tales of valour, of love, and of light.
In the heart of the wilderness, under the arctic dome,
the magic fire in the sky, forever calls us home.

So when you see them shimmer, hear their silent cry,
know it's nature's symphony, painting the sky.
For in those fleeting moments, as the colours fly,
you're witnessing the magic, the fire in the sky.

Juxtaposition

Beneath the canvas of an amber sky,
nature's portrait painted, a lullaby.
Where untouched landscapes whisper tales,
and rolling green hills sway in timeless gales.

Yet, in this ballad of Earth's refrain,
a discordant note, a haunting pain.
Man's imprint, a scar on the virgin land,
the consequence of an indifferent hand.

Behold the forest, once a cathedral grand,
now echoes with the logger's demand.
Timber's plunder, a relentless siege,
leaving hollow echoes, a silent dirge.

Mountains that once pierced the heavens high,
now bear the wounds of strip-mining's sigh.
Their majesty marred by avarice untamed,
as the Earth weeps, its beauty maimed.

Rivers that once danced with pure delight,
choked by debris, a grievous plight.
The waters weep, as the currents wane,
a tragic elegy, a mournful strain.

Yet, in the heart of the desolate scene,
whispers persist, the land's hopeful sheen.
For in the untouched corners that remain,
a plea lingers, a call to abstain.

In valleys where untouched beauty thrives,
the urgency of conservation arrives.
Let not progress be a ruthless foe,
but a steward of Earth, a mindful bow.

The juxtaposition of beauty and decay,
a stark reminder, day by day.
Timeless landscapes, a fragile grace,
in the hands of humanity, a delicate embrace.

Awake, stewards of this fragile Earth,
for in this tapestry of death and birth,
conservation weaves a hopeful thread,
a promise to heal what greed has bled.

Let the winds of change be winds of care,
to nurture the land, not strip it bare.
For in the juxtaposition of what was and what could be,
lies the choice to protect Earth's legacy.

Ocean's Child

Beneath the azure veil, where dreams are spun,
the ocean cradles her child, the eternal one.
Born of the tides, in a celestial trance,
an offspring of wonder, in the ocean's expanse.

With frothy kisses on the shore's embrace,
the ocean's child emerges, a figure of grace.
Eyes as deep as the abyss, reflecting the sky,
a whispered lullaby in every wave's sigh.

Hair of seaweed, a verdant crown,
in the underwater kingdom, where mysteries drown.
Fingers that ripple like currents below,
in the realm of Poseidon, where currents bestow.

In the moonlit ripples and the sunlit gleam,
the ocean's child, a shimmering dream.
With a laugh that echoes through coral halls,
a symphony of life, where the ocean calls.

The child of Neptune, with scales that gleam,
navigates the depths like a watery dream.
A guardian spirit in the watery wild,
born of the sea, the ocean's own child.

A dance with dolphins, a chorus with whales,
in the ocean's embrace, where love prevails.
A timeless kinship, a watery bond,
in the liquid arms, where mysteries respond.

So, in the ebb and flow, in the salt-kissed air,
the ocean's child dances without a care.
Born of the waves, in the depths beguiled,
a maritime sprite, the ocean's own child.

Kākerōri Fly

Dedicated to the Rarotonga monarch or Rarotonga flycatcher, endemic to the Cook Islands and currently listed as vulnerable with around 700 birds alive. It came back from being critically endangered and on the brink of extinction after only 29 birds existed in the wild in 1989.

In the heart of Polynesia, where the ocean's embrace is warm,
I am the voice of an ancient soul, weathered and worn.
I am the Kākerōri, once a symphony in flight,
now whispers in the wind, a fading beacon of light.

Beneath the palm fronds, where shadows dance with grace,
I unfold my tale, a melancholy embrace.
With feathers that once painted the sky in hues,
I soar through legends, where once I chose.

In lands where the sun kisses the Pacific shore,
I fluttered freely, wings of folklore.
But the human tide, relentless, swept ashore,
a wave of change, and I was cast ashore.

Listen, oh kin of Earth, to my plaintive plea,
a Kākerōri's lament, a call from the sea.
I speak of hopes that bloomed in emerald green,
now wither in shadows, unseen, unheard, unseen.

Once, the forest echoed with my melodic song,
a rhythm ancient, where I did belong.
Yet now, the echoes wane, the melody declines,
silent whispers carried by the ocean winds.

Through thickets and canopies, my journey unfurled,
a testament to life in this Polynesian world.
Yet now, each footfall, a thunderous drum,
disrupts my dance, leaves my spirit numb.

Rising tides, encroaching woes, a tempest on the rise,
as human shadows cast darkness in our skies.
The trappings of progress, a perilous parade,
my paradise lost, in the footsteps humans made.

I yearn for the days when coconuts cradled the
breeze,
and fragrant blossoms floated through the trees.
Now, bulldozers hum, a discordant symphony,
and I, the Kākerōri, almost faded into history.

Oceans of plastic, the islands drift apart,
yet in this sea of sorrow, beats a hopeful heart.
Hear my cry, ye stewards of land and sea,
redeem the pledge, restore my sanctuary.

For in the folds of your hands lies my fate,
the power to alter this perilous state.
Let my wings once again paint the azure sky,
and in the heart of Polynesia, let the Kākerōri fly.

The Ballad of Nature's Tears

In a world once green and vast,
where rivers flowed, and forests cast
their shadows long, and skies so clear,
humans came, with hope and fear.

Oh, the tales of old we hear,
of nature's cry, so pure, so clear.
For every stone that we did turn,
a lesson learned, a scar to burn.

Mountains tall, they reached the skies,
witnessed the tears, heard the cries.
For every tree that we did fell,
a whispered tale, a silent spell.

Oh, the tales of old we weave,
of promises made, yet hard to believe.
For every meadow turned to grey,
a price we'll pay, come what may.

Stars above, they watch in sorrow,
as we borrow from tomorrow.
Rivers once so full and grand,
now drift upon the desert sand.

Creatures of the wild, they flee,
from the world changed, from the sea to sea.
For every songbird that did flee,
a lost melody, a plea to be free.

Oh, the tales we now recall,
of nature's rise, and our great fall.
For in our quest, in our grand stride,
nature wept, as we cast aside.

Yet hope remains, a flicker, a spark,
in the quiet of the forest, the lonely lark.
For if we listen, if we truly hear,
nature's song, so crystal clear.

Oh, the tales yet to unfold,
of a future written, of stories yet untold.
May we learn, may we find a way,
to mend the bond, to finally sway.

In the dance of time, as days go by,
may we cherish, may we rectify.
For in our hands, the power does lie,
to heal the earth, to let it fly.

Printed by Libri Plureos GmbH in Hamburg,
Germany